Did Yo

SHEF

A MISCELLANY

Compiled by Julia Skinner

With particular reference to the work of Clive Hardy and Melvyn Jones

THE FRANCIS FRITH COLLECTION

www.francisfrith.com

Based on a book first published in the United Kingdom in 2006 by The Francis Frith Collection®

This edition published exclusively for Identity Books in 2010 ISBN 978-1-84589-385-9

British Library Cataloguing in Publication Data

Did You Know? Sheffield - A Miscellany
Compiled by Julia Skinner
With particular reference to the work of Clive Hardy and Melvyn Jones

The Francis Frith Collection
Frith's Barn, Teffont,
Salisbury, Wiltshire SP3 5QP
Tel: +44 (0) 1722 716 376
Email: info@francisfrith.co.uk
www.francisfrith.com

Printed and bound in Malaysia

Front Cover: **SHEFFIELD, FITZALAN SQUARE 1902** 48268p

The colour-tinting is for illustrative purposes only, and is not intended to be historically accurate

AS WITH ANY HISTORICAL DATABASE, THE FRANCIS FRITH ARCHIVE IS CONSTANTLY BEING CORRECTED AND IMPROVED, AND THE PUBLISHERS WOULD WELCOME INFORMATION ON OMISSIONS OR INACCURACIES

CONTENTS

INTRODUCTION

Sheffield has been famous since the 14th century for making cutlery, but it was local clock maker Benjamin Huntsman's discovery in the 18th century that steel could be purified by using a crucible that led to Sheffield becoming the steel capital of Britain. Forges, metal-working shops and steelworks in the area came in all shapes and sizes, from those employing just a handful of men to the industrial giants like Firth Brown and Hadfields. There were other important industries in Sheffield too, such as the Yorkshire Engine Co, which built railway locomotives, and there were also several collieries within easy reach of the city centre.

Sheffield was badly damaged during the Second World War, particularly on the night and early morning of 12-13 December and the night of 15 December 1940. There was heavy damage to property, with 2,849 houses being totally demolished. Civilian deaths amounted to 668 and another 513 were seriously injured. Following the wartime devastation much of the city centre was rebuilt. Little now survives of the pre-Victorian era, save for parts of the cathedral and a handful of houses.

In the second half of the 20th century foreign competition in the cutlery industry was affecting Sheffield's trade, not only from the traditional rivals of the USA, France and Germany but also from the Far East and South Korea. The crash came in the 1970s, and most of Sheffield's great names disappeared. Viners, the largest cutlery firm in the country, went out of business in 1982; its name and trademark were sold, and now they appear on imported Korean cutlery. The silver and electro-plate companies fared no better, and the workshops and factories of many of the traditional old Sheffield companies have been demolished, or converted for new uses. Sheffield's heavy steel industry also went into severe decline in the late 1970s and early 1980s. Employment in the steel works in the Lower Don Valley declined from 40,000 in the mid 1970s to 13,000 ten years later.

However, the Lower Don Valley was rejuvenated in the closing years of the 20th century. It now contains, for example, a renovated canal basin (renamed Victoria Quays), a technology park, the Don Valley

Stadium (the biggest athletics stadium in the country), the Arena which holds 12,000 people, and the Meadowhall shopping centre with 270 stores and parking for 12,000 cars.

'Smoky Sheffield' is now a thing of the past. The 21st-century city is an attractive and confident place in which to live and work. After the decline of its traditional industries in the 1970s and 1980s, Sheffield has now turned the corner with a much more varied economy and with large parts of its townscape regenerated and renewed. The £130m Heart of the City scheme is revitalising Sheffield's city centre. It has already seen the opening of the Millennium Galleries, the Winter Garden and the re-designing of the Peace Gardens, and the transformation of the entry into Sheffield outside the railway station by the creation of a new public plaza with water features and a 90m-long steel sculpture representing a knife blade will ensure that the city's proud industrial heritage is never forgotten.

THE STRADDLE WAREHOUSE, VICTORIA QUAYS 2005 S108713

SOUTH YORKSHIRE DIALECT WORDS AND PHRASES

'Well, I'll go to the foot o' our stairs!' - I'm really surprised!

'Clemmed' - very cold, frozen through.

'Nesh' - feeling the cold, as in ***'I'm a bit nesh'***.

'Laykin' - skiving off school or work.

'Mardy' - peevish, querulous, miserable, moody, sulking.

'Snicket' - a pathway, between hedges, fences etc.

'I'm stood 'ere like Clem Alice!' - I'm standing here waiting, looking like a complete idiot!

'It's a bit black over Bill's mother's' - It looks like it might rain.

A mother's complaint to a child:
'Where's tha bin tha mucky tyke
Laykin t'all afternoon
Inter't sink oil yor'll be fun
Look at tha britches showin
Muck an splat reet up t'neck
Black as soot thee clothes
No more laykin for thee tonait
Inter t'outhouse tha guz begone.'

The Yorkshire version of the 'See No Evil, Hear No Evil' saying:
'See all
Hear all
Say nowt

Eyt all
Sup all
Pay nowt

An' if tha does owt for nowt,
Do it for thissen'.

HAUNTED SHEFFIELD

There are many ghost stories in Sheffield, and one of the best ways to find out about them is to go on one of the organised ghost walks that take place regularly around the city. For more information see: www.steelcityghosttours.co.uk

One of the city's most famous ghosts is said to be that of Mary, Queen of Scots, who haunts the Turret House of Sheffield Manor Lodge (see photograph S108703 on page 11), where she spent part of her long period of captivity in the reign of Elizabeth I. There have been several reported sightings of a beautiful lady dressed in black, who seems to glide across the floor and disappear through walls, and a dog that once lived in the house was said to be particularly sensitive to the ghostly presence, and became distressed if left in the house alone. The queen's ghostly face is said to sometimes be seen looking out from a window of the Turret House.

The title of Sheffield's most haunted pub is claimed by Carbrook Hall at Attercliffe Common. Psychic investigations have identified one of the resident ghosts as Colonel John Bright, a Parliamentarian soldier from the time of the Civil War in the 17th century - although he is said to be a peaceful, benevolent spirit. Colonel Bright was a real person who once lived in the Hall, and rode to York to ask for artillery support during the Civil War, when Sheffield Castle was about to be taken by Royalist forces. Amongst a number of other ghosts alleged to haunt the pub are an elderly woman, a monk, and another Parliamentarian soldier from the Civil War period. A mysterious shadowy entity is also said to haunt the bar, sometimes throwing items around.

Several strange events were reported when the Stocksbridge Bypass on the A616 north-west of Sheffield was being built in the 1980s. Many workmen said that they had seen a group of mysterious children dressed in old-fashioned clothes on the site at night, singing, dancing and playing, but there were no traces of their footsteps in the muddy ground the next day. Another strange apparition that is supposed to haunt the area of the bypass is that of a monk, and a clairvoyant has claimed that the contractors who built the road disturbed the monk's grave during its construction. The bypass was recently claimed to be the second most haunted road in Britain by the Paranormal Research Foundation.

SHEFFIELD MISCELLANY

Sheffield is in the old West Riding of Yorkshire. It was the Viking Danes who first divided the huge county of Yorkshire into the ridings, or 'thridings' - thirds - and they became the North, East and West Ridings before local government reorganisation in 1974.

Sheffield began life as a town rather than a village in the late 11th century, under its Norman lords. Following the Norman Conquest of 1066, King William ordered a great survey to be made of the wealth of his new lands, which became known as the Domesday Book. In what was to become the parish of Sheffield, Sheffield itself, Hallam (recorded as Hallun), Attercliffe and Darnall were recorded for the first time, as was Grimeshou, later changed to Grimesthorpe. In neighbouring Ecclesfield parish (which together with Sheffield parish became known as Hallamshire), besides Ecclesfield itself the Domesday Book also recorded Holdworth above the Loxley Valley, Ughill, Worrall and what today is the tiny hamlet of Onesacre. Other places beyond Hallamshire but now within the city boundaries were recorded in the Domesday survey, including Tinsley and the villages formerly in Derbyshire - Beighton, Mosborough, Norton, Totley and Dore.

Barker's Pool is so named because this is where a man called Barker made a pool in the 15th century for the storage of water collected from several springs on the hillside above West Bar. Barker's Pool was in fact little more than a pond, and was condemned as a public nuisance in 1793 and filled in.

HIGH STREET 1900 45485

BARKER'S POOL c1955 S108055

HIGH STREET c1960 S108110

The Norman town of Sheffield was established immediately to the south-west of the confluence of the Rivers Don and Sheaf. The first castle at Sheffield dates from the 12th century when the Norman lord, William de Lovetot, built a motte and bailey castle. The two rivers formed a natural moat to the castle on the north and east. In the second half of the 13th century this castle was destroyed by fire during the barons' revolt, and replaced by a stone castle. During the Civil War the castle was garrisoned for the king, but was surrendered to Parliament in 1644. The castle was largely demolished on Cromwell's orders in the late 1640s, after which it was plundered for building stone by local people. A few remains of the castle survive in the basement of the Castle Market.

The medieval market town of Sheffield grew up under the protection of its castle. In 1281 Thomas de Furnival was asked by a royal enquiry into the rights of landowners (called 'Quo Warranto') on what grounds he believed he had the right to hold a market in Sheffield, and he replied that his ancestors had held it since the Norman Conquest. He put this right to hold a market on a more formal footing fifteen years later when in 1296 he obtained a royal charter for a market every Tuesday and a fair at the Feast of Holy Trinity, which fell in either May or June.

FARGATE c1955 S108006

Beneath Sheffield's castle walls lay the oldest part of the medieval town, in a tight cluster of narrow streets including what is the modern Market Place, Haymarket (formerly called the Beast Market and before that the Bull Stake), Waingate (formerly called Bridge Street), Castle Green, Castle Folds, Dixon Lane, Snig Hill, and the now lost Pudding Lane, Water Lane and Truelove's Gutter (which was also an open sewer). Surviving documents from the late 16th century give the impression of a tightly-knit collection of houses, cottages and shops with their outbuildings, gardens, crofts and yards. Before the 17th century nearly all the houses in the town would have been timber-framed.

The medieval expansion of Sheffield along High Street and Fargate is revealed by the long narrow building plots. They are sometimes separated by long narrow lanes such as Change Alley, Mulberry Street and Chapel Walk. They developed in this way so that as many workshops and shop owners as possible could have a commercial frontage on the main streets.

The first stone bridge in Sheffield, Lady's Bridge, was built across the River Don in 1486. It is named after the Chapel of Our Blessed Lady of the Bridge which stood to the south of the river. This late medieval bridge, which is hidden below the modern bridge, attests to the outstanding craftsmanship of its builder, William Hyll, who had been instructed to 'make a sufficient brigge over the watry of Dune neghe the castell of Sheffield'.

THE TURRET HOUSE, SHEFFIELD MANOR LODGE 2005 S108703

Mary, Queen of Scots was held captive in Sheffield in the charge of the 6th Earl of Shrewsbury from 1570 until 1584. She was moved from the castle from time to time to Sheffield Manor Lodge (see photograph S108703, above). Elizabeth I's ministers were concerned that she might escape from this less fortified residence, but the earl's son assured them that 'unless she could transform herself into a flea or a mouse' it would be impossible for her to do so.

THE CATHEDRAL c1955 S108035

Sheffield's original parish church of St Peter and St Paul was built in the 12th century, and rebuilt again in the late medieval period. In January 1898 the Privy Council gave its approval for Sheffield to have its own bishopric. However a few months later the Archbishop of York ordered the scheme to be abandoned on the grounds that 'it would not be desirable to proceed for some years to come'. It was not until March 1914 that the church was granted cathedral status, and Dr Hedley Burrows was invested as the first Bishop of Sheffield and enthroned at the cathedral on 1 May 1914.

Sheffield's cathedral is famed for its Shrewsbury Chapel, which is located on the south side of the 15th-century chancel; among the monuments is one to the 6th Earl of Shrewsbury, who was burdened for many years with the task of looking after Mary, Queen of Scots during her long period of captivity in England (see photograph S108701, below). The figure of the earl has his head resting on a cushion and his feet on a dog, called a Talbot, a breed of hound used in tracking and hunting.

THE CATHEDRAL, THE TOMB OF GEORGE TALBOT, 6TH EARL OF SHREWSBURY 2005 S108701

The first time that Sheffield's cutlery industry was referred to in documents was in the tax returns of 1297. In those returns Robertus le coteler - Robert the cutler - was listed as a taxpayer. By Elizabethan times Sheffield was second only to London in cutlery manufacture, and in 1540 John Leland, the topographical writer, wrote that 'ther be many smiths and cutlers in Hallamshire'.

The Company of Cutlers in Hallamshire came into being though an Act of Parliament in 1624. At the time of the passing of the Act there were 498 master craftsmen in Sheffield and the surrounding villages: 440 knife makers, 31 shear and sickle makers, and 27 scissor makers.

The existence of fast-flowing rivers gave Sheffield and surrounding parishes a great industrial advantage over rival centres. There were about 50 water-powered industrial sites on Sheffield's rivers by 1660; the number had risen to about 90 by 1740 and to about 130 by the end of the 18th century. Water-power on the rivers was harnessed in the same way for centuries. A weir was built to deflect water from the river into a reservoir (called a dam) via an artificial channel called a head goit. Water was led from the dam onto a vertical water wheel and then flowed back into the river via a channel called a tail goit.

THE VICTORIA (METHODIST) HALL c1955 S108004

THE TRAM TERMINUS c1870 S108002a

Old Sheffield Plate, as plated silver became known, was invented by a cutler called Thomas Boulsover (1704-88), when he was repairing a knife handle made of silver and copper. He realised that a thin sheet of silver could be fused together with copper to give the impression of solid silver - and a new Sheffield trade was born. Boulsover had to roll and craft his plated silver by hand, but soon other firms were entering the trade. During the 18th century firms such as John Hoyland & Co, Joseph Hancock, and Tudor, Leader & Sherburn became major manufacturers of a wide range of plated silver articles such as snuff boxes, pocket flasks, buckles, buttons, candlesticks, and a wide range of fancy 'holloware' such as coffee pots, jugs, dishes, bowls and trays.

Crucible steel, which resulted in the growing international reputation of Sheffield as a steel-making centre, was developed by a clock maker, Benjamin Huntsman, in the 1740s. He was dissatisfied with the quality of steel available to him for making clock springs so he experimented in producing a homogenous steel without variations in its carbon content. Crucible steel is so called because it was manufactured by putting broken bars of blister steel in small clay pots (crucibles) in a coke fire at very high temperatures for up to five hours. The end result was the ideal steel for cutlery and edge tool making, and by the 1850s around 90% of the country's crucible steel was made in Sheffield, as well as nearly 50% of all the steel made in Europe.

THE GOODWIN FOUNTAIN c1965 S108173

A CEMENTATION FURNACE, HOYLE STREET 2005 S108705

By the mid 17th century Sheffield's industry was run by master craftsmen called 'little mesters' who ran their own businesses with the help of apprentices and journeymen (workers who had completed their apprenticeships but had not set up their own firms) from small workshops attached to their cottages or at water-powered grinding wheels. Here might be a coal-fuelled smithy where blades were forged or small rooms where the handles were fitted or 'hafted', and where knives were finally assembled after the blades had been taken to a riverside cutlers' wheel to be ground on a grindstone. Some cutlers might specialise in forging, grinding or assembling.

Until the second half of the 18th century the steel used by Sheffield's cutlers was either imported or was locally made 'shear steel' which was forged from 'blister steel' made in a cementation furnace. Some 260 such furnaces, easily recognised by their conical chimneys, were eventually built in the Sheffield area; photograph S108705, opposite, shows the only remaining cementation furnace in Sheffield, on Hoyle Street.

Fortunes were made by the heads of Sheffield's light steel firms in the American trade in the first half of the 19th century. For this reason some firms went as far as naming their new works with American-style titles - for instance, George Wostenholm's factory was known as the Washington Cutlery Works, and Alfred Beckett's saw works was the Brooklyn Saw Works (see photograph S108720 on page 51).

The adoption of the Bessemer process, invented by Henry Bessemer, revolutionised steel making in Sheffield in the 1860s. Using traditional methods of converting pig iron into blister steel and then into crucible steel took 14 or 15 days to produce a 40-50lb ingot of cast steel, whereas the Bessemer process could produce 6 tons of cast steel in about 30 minutes. The Bessemer converter made its first appearance on Carlisle Street at Bessemer's Steel Works in 1858. Two of Sheffield's major new firms, John Brown's and Charles Cammell's, became the earliest to use the new process and produced their first Bessemer steel rails in 1861, followed by Samuel Fox in 1863.

After 1880 specialisation became a key feature of Sheffield's heavy steel industry, and the research laboratory became very important. One of the most brilliant applied scientists in Sheffield was Sir Robert Hadfield (1858-1940). In 1883 at the age of only 25 he took out his first patent for non-magnetic silicon steel, which was used for tramway and railway points. Stainless steel was discovered in Sheffield in 1913 by Harry Brearley, director of Brown-Firth's research laboratories. Brearley came from a poor Sheffield background having been born in Ramsden's Yard off the Wicker, and was presented with the Freedom of the City in 1939.

A cholera epidemic hit Sheffield in July 1832, and by December 402 of the inhabitants had died from the disease. Cholera is an intestinal infection, and is particularly rife where the water supply is polluted. Most of the dead were from the poorer end of society, but the disease was no respecter of social rank - it also claimed one of Sheffield's leading citizens, John Blake, Master Cutler. Burial of the dead in public graveyards was forbidden after 8 August, and from then on burials took place in a special burial ground on Norfolk Road, where in 1834 the Cholera Monument was erected (see photograph S108707, opposite).

THE CHOLERA MONUMENT 2005 S108707

THE TOWN HALL c1955 S108012

Major changes took place in Sheffield in the second half of the 19th century, probably in connection with it being recognised as a city in 1893. The development had begun in the 1840s when the Town Trustees began getting involved in road-widening schemes, including those at Snig Hill, Tenter Street, Trippet Lane and Figtree Lane. In 1875 the town centre was redeveloped with the construction of Pinstone Street, Leopold Street and Surrey Street, and in 1893 the council began a slum clearance programme in the Crofts, an area extending from the rear of the parish church to West Bar. Plans were also drawn up for the erection of a new Town Hall befitting one of the newest cities in the kingdom (see photograph 37422, opposite).

Sheffield's gabled, Renaissance-style Town Hall, built on the corner of Pinstone Street and Surrey Street, was designed by E W Mountford; it was completed in 1896, and opened by Queen Victoria in 1897. The tower is 210ft high and topped off with a bronze statue by Mario Raggi of Vulcan, a large nude figure holding a hammer in his right hand and arrows in his left, with his right foot resting on an anvil - apparently the figure for the statue was modelled by a Life Guardsman.

THE TOWN HALL 1896 37422

The Corporation had taken over the tramway system in Sheffield in 1896 and lost no time in converting it from horse to electric traction - electric street tramcars were introduced into Sheffield in 1899, and in photograph 48268, below, we see

FITZALAN SQUARE 1902 48268

a selection of single-deckers and open-top double-deckers. The single-deck trams were used on routes with low railway bridges. Note also in this view the wooden stalls used as tramway stops.

FARGATE 1893 31961

Photograph 31961, above, shows Fargate, the heart of the city centre; all this is now pedestrianised. The Albany Hotel, dating from the late 1870s, was originally a Temperance establishment. The YMCA building to the left of the complex was added in 1891. The frontage of the hotel has now changed, with the removal of the top windows and decoration. The obelisk seen in the photograph commemorated Queen Victoria's golden jubilee in 1887; it was removed to Endcliffe Woods in 1903 and a statue of Queen Victoria replaced it here in 1905, but this was also taken to the woods in 1930.

The Sheffield & South Yorkshire Canal, from the basin to Tinsley, was completed in 1819. It joined the much older Don Navigation and from there went to the Stainforth & Keaby Canal, offering Sheffield manufacturers a link with the navigable River Trent and access to the ports of Hull and Grimsby. In 1905 the newly completed New Junction Canal provided a link between the Don, the Aire & Calder Navigation, and the port of Goole. Photograph S108001, below, shows several barges at the phenomenally busy Canal Basin, loaded with scrap metal en route for reprocessing. The canal came right into the heart of the city, close to the Corn Exchange. Everything in this photograph has changed now. The Basin is now Victoria Quays, and leisure development has become all important. The Great Central Railway sidings to the right of the photograph have also disappeared.

THE CANAL BASIN 1870 S108001

BARKER'S POOL c1965 S108116

In the centre of photograph S108116, above, is the Gaumont cinema, which opened as the Regent in 1927; to the right is Cole Brothers' department store. Also featured in this view is the Sheffield War Memorial, designed by Charles Carus Wilson and unveiled in October 1925. In the early days of the First World War young men from certain districts were told that if they all joined up together they would be able to serve together, in battalions that became known as 'Pals'. Sheffield formed a 'Pals' battalion, the Sheffield City Battalion, which fought alongside the Accrington 'Pals' on 1 July 1916, the first day of the Somme offensive, to capture the village of Serre. Unfortunately the nature of the 'Pals' system meant that large numbers of men from one area who served and fought together would often also die together, and the Sheffield City Battalion was almost annihilated at this action - when the surviving members of the battalion were taken out of the line on 3 July, 513 officers and men had been killed or seriously wounded, or were missing in action. The novel 'A Covenant with Death' by John Harris tells the story of a recruit who joined the Sheffield City Battalion, and describes the attack on Serre in the poignant words: 'Two years in the making. Ten minutes in the destroying. That was our history'.

Photograph S108015, below, shows the City Hall, which was designed by E Vincent Harris in the Classical style featuring a Corinthian columned entrance; it was built using Darley Dale stone, and was completed in 1932. It was originally conceived as a memorial hall to the Sheffield people who died in the First World War. Inside is the Oval Hall, where up to 2,800 people can be seated for concerts. The front of the hall still bears the scars of the night during the Second World War when a bomb landed to the side of the War Memorial (shown on the right of the photograph).

THE CITY HALL c1955 S108015

Sheffield's High Street was one of the principal shopping areas of the city to be damaged during the air raids of the Second World War. In December 1940 the front of the C&A store collapsed into the street following three direct hits, and around 70 people died in the Marples Hotel when it too took a direct hit and was destroyed.

Sheffield's heavy steel industry made a massive contribution to the war effort in the two World Wars. At the outset of the First World War Sheffield was described as 'the greatest armoury the world has ever seen'. In the first 18 months of the Second World War the only drop hammer in the country capable of forging Spitfire crankshafts was at the Vickers' River Don works.

The photographs in this book that were taken from the 1950s onwards show something of the rebuilding and redevelopment of Sheffield following its wartime devastation. Photograph S108222, opposite top, shows a view of Park Hill, towering above the Sheffield Midland Station. When Park Hill was built it was hailed by sociologists, architects and planners as being one of the country's most significant housing schemes - but these people did not have to live in it. Even though Park Hill won the Department of Environment Design in Housing Award in 1967, its residents soon christened the place 'San Quentin', after the notorious jail in the USA. The housing development is now a Grade II* listed building, and a major refurbishment programme is planned to transform the complex into up-market apartments and small business premises.

Photograph S108221, opposite below, shows the then brand new Polytechnic, which was formed in 1969 with the amalgamation of the Sheffield Colleges of Technology and Art; the new institution was housed in purpose-built facilities on land between Howard Street and Pond Street.

THE SHEFFIELD MIDLAND STATION AND PARK HILL c1965 S108222

THE POLYTECHNIC c1969 S108221

Shown in photograph S108049, below, are the original university buildings at Western Bank, built between 1903 and 1905. The university was an amalgamation of three earlier institutions, the Sheffield School of Medicine, the Firth College and the Technical School. When the university opened for business in 1905 it had just 100 full-time students. By the mid 1960s the university had embarked on an ambitious expansion programme complemented with an equally impressive building scheme. The university library, seen in photograph S108181, opposite, is considered to be one of the finest post-Second World War buildings in the city.

THE UNIVERSITY c1955 S108049

THE UNIVERSITY c1965 S108181

Just before midnight on 11 March 1864 a major disaster struck Sheffield. The Dale Dyke Reservoir collapsed and the waters of the reservoir burst down the Lockley Valley towards Sheffield, eight miles away. The crushing torrent of 114 million cubic feet of water swept everything before it - cottages, farm buildings, water-powered mills, bridges, livestock and people. The waters swept on, unstoppable, down the Don Valley into central Sheffield. 240 people were drowned, 415 houses and 106 works and shops were completely or partially destroyed, and 15 stone bridges were swept away.

In 1930 the Ecclesall Union Hospital came under local government control and was renamed Nether Edge. The institution had an interesting history. When it opened as a workhouse in 1842 there was no segregation of the poor, sick or insane. They were all

NETHER EDGE HOSPITAL c1955 S108081

housed together, and would remain so until 1865, when special wards for infectious diseases and what were then referred to as lunatics were established in a new block. The building, shown in photograph S108081, below, was converted to housing in 2000-03.

BEAUCHIEF, THE ABBEY c1950 B335014

THE MAPPIN ART GALLERY 1893 31968

Beauchief is four miles south of Sheffield, but all that remains of the Premonstratensian abbey founded by Robert Fitz Ranulf around 1183 is the west tower, seen in photograph B335014, opposite above. Around 1662 a small chapel dedicated to St Thomas Becket was built against the east wall of the tower; many of its fittings, including the pulpit, Communion table and box pews, date from the 1660s.

Photograph 31968, opposite below, shows the Mappin Art Gallery in Weston Park in 1893. All but the façade and two front galleries of the building seen in this view were destroyed by bombing in 1940. The Mappin Art Gallery and the attached City Museum have recently undergone a £20m Heritage Lottery-funded renovation, and the complex is now known as the Weston Park Museum. The museum contains a collection of cutlery dating from the 16th century and the world's finest collection of Sheffield plate. As well as hosting a permanent collection of British art, the Mappin also displays loan exhibitions from the extensive collection belonging to the Graves Art Gallery in the centre of Sheffield.

The Crucible Theatre, opened in 1971, has gained Sheffield a new national and international reputation - but not for theatrical productions on its thrust stage or in its studio theatre. It is best known as the venue for the annual World Snooker Championships.

THE PEACE GARDENS AND THE TOWN HALL c1965 S108178

Building work on St Paul's Church in Sheffield began in 1720, but the church did not open for services until 1740 because of a dispute between the church authorities and John Downes, the main donor of the money for its construction, about whose responsibility it was to appoint the curate. The church was demolished in 1938 and the site was cleared in the same year to create the open space known as the Peace Gardens, which were named to commemorate the peace that was misguidedly expected from the Munich Agreement of that year. The gardens were redesigned in 1997-98.

In Weston Park is the statue of the poet Ebenezer Elliott, seen in photograph 31970x, below, which originally stood in the Market Place. Born at Masbrough in 1781, Elliott moved to Sheffield following the failure of his father's business. He is famous for his Corn Law rhymes - he considered the Corn Laws to be an obscenity as they kept the price of bread artificially high - and his work had many admirers, including William Wordsworth, who said 'None of us have done better than he has in his best'. Elliott also composed verses about Sheffield and the surrounding townships, including 'Farewell to Rivilin', where he describes his regret at leaving a favourite spot by a Sheffield stream when he moved away from the area.

WESTON PARK, EBENEZER ELLIOTT'S STATUE 1893 31970x

For many centuries the ancient woods around Sheffield provided charcoal, the original fuel used for iron and steel making. Sheffield still has a unique woodland resource - it is the best-wooded city in the country, with about 80 ancient woods (ie known to have existed before the year 1600) within its boundaries. In 1999 a Heritage Lottery bid to restore 35 ancient woodlands in Sheffield, Rotherham and Barnsley was successful. The project is called 'Fuelling a Revolution - the woods that founded the steel country', and was awarded £1.5m so that the region's woodland heritage can be actively managed and interpreted for schools and the general public.

ENDCLIFFE WOODS 1893 31976

SPORTING SHEFFIELD

Sheffield can claim to be the home of the world's two oldest football clubs. Sheffield FC was founded in 1857 and is still in existence, playing its games at the Don Valley Stadium. Hallam FC was founded just three years later and is also still in existence, playing its matches at its original ground, Sandygate. Hallam FC took part in what was probably the first football tournament under the modern rules, the Youdan Cup, held in the city in 1867. Hallam FC won the final, which was played at Bramall Lane.

Bramall Lane, home of Sheffield United Football Club, is thought to be the oldest major ground which still hosts professional football matches. It also has the distinction of being one of only two grounds to have staged an England cricket match against Australia, an England football international, and an FA Cup final. The Oval in London is the other. Sheffield United Football Club achieved promotion to the Premier League at the end of the 2005/06 season.

The name of Sheffield Wednesday Football Club was originally 'the Wednesday Cricket Club'. A cricket team of that name was established in the early 19th century and later a football team was set up in association with it. For many years the football club was known as 'The Wednesday', before its official name was changed to Sheffield Wednesday FC in the late 1920s.

Sheffield is fortunate to have a number of top class sporting arenas, including Bramall Lane, Hillsborough and the Don Valley Stadium. The Don Valley Stadium was built to be ready for the World Student Games in 1991, and was at that time the first brand new major sporting arena built in England since Wembley stadium. It remains Britain's biggest athletics stadium with some of the best facilities, including the country's strongest floodlights.

QUIZ QUESTIONS

Answers on page 48.

1. What does the name 'Sheffield' mean?

2. In 1912 a memorial concert was held in Endcliffe Woods to raise funds for which disaster appeal?

3. What was 'rattening'?

4. What does the word 'snig' mean in the street name 'Snig Hill'?

5. In 'The Reeve's Tale' of Chaucer's 'The Canterbury Tales', a character is mentioned carrying a 'Scheffeld thwitel'. What was this?

6. What was the name used in Sheffield for the covered passage that linked back-to-back houses facing the street with those in the courtyard behind?

7. What is Butcher's Wheel in Sheffield, and why is it important?

8. What is 'crozzle'?

9. What is the name of Sheffield's ice-hockey team?

10. On top of Sheffield's Town Hall is a statue of Vulcan. Vulcan has been associated with the city for many years, and appears as a supporter on Sheffield's coat of arms - but who was Vulcan?

FARGATE c1955 S108005

RECIPE

YORKSHIRE CURD TART

The distinguishing and traditional characteristic of Yorkshire Curd Tart is allspice (or 'clove pepper' as it was also known), but mixed spice can be substituted for the ground allspice if this flavour is preferred.

Ingredients

For the pastry:
115g/4oz butter, diced
225g/8oz plain flour
1 egg yolk

For the filling:
A large pinch of ground allspice (or mixed spice)
3 eggs, beaten
90g/3½oz soft light brown sugar
Grated rind and juice of 1 lemon
40g/1½oz melted butter
450g/1lb curd cheese, or cottage cheese if curd cheese is hard to find
75g/3oz raisins or sultanas

Preheat the oven to 190 degrees C/375 degrees F/Gas Mark 5.

To make the pastry - rub the butter into the flour until the mixture resembles fine breadcrumbs. Stir the egg yolk into the flour mixture with a little water to bind the dough together. Turn the dough on to a lightly floured surface, knead lightly and form into a ball. Roll out the pastry thinly and use to line a 20cm/8in fluted loose-bottomed flan tin. Chill for 15 minutes.

To make the filling - mix the ground allspice (or mixed spice) with the sugar, then stir in the eggs, lemon rind and juice, butter, curd or cottage cheese and dried fruit. Pour the filling into the chilled pastry case, then bake in the preheated oven for about 40 minutes until the pastry is cooked and the filling is lightly set and golden brown. Serve still slightly warm, cut into wedges, with cream.

ANGEL STREET c1965 S108175

THE STEEL GIANT SCULPTURE, BOWDEN HOUSTEADS WOOD 2005 S108710

RECIPE

YORKSHIRE BUN LOAF

Ingredients

275g/10oz self-raising flour
100g/4oz margarine
75g/3oz caster sugar
2 eggs, beaten
2 teaspoons marmalade
75g/3oz sultanas
75g/3oz currants
A little milk

Sift the flour into a bowl. Rub in the margarine, then stir in the sugar, eggs, marmalade, sultanas and currants. Bind to a medium stiff mixture with milk, then turn into a greased 500g/1lb loaf tin. Sprinkle the top with caster sugar and bake in a preheated moderately hot oven (190 degrees C/375 degrees F/Gas Mark 5) for 1 hour.

Store the loaf in an airtight tin, and serve in slices spread with butter.

QUIZ ANSWERS

1. The name Sheffield testifies to the well-wooded character of the area in Saxon and early medieval times. Sheffield means 'a treeless area in an otherwise well-wooded area (-feld) beside the River Sheaf'. The Anglo-Saxon place-name element of -feld also occurs in the local names of Ballifield, Bradfield, Ecclesfield and Hallfield.

2. In 1912 a memorial concert was held in Endcliffe Woods in aid of the Titanic Disaster Fund.

3. 'Rattening', which originally referred to rats destroying human belongings, took on a more sinister meaning during the 'Sheffield Outrages' of the second half of the 19th century, when trade unionists were accused of threatening non-union members by means of arson, intimidation and murder. It became the term used for the confiscation of a workman's tools on behalf of trade societies to persuade workers to join a union, pay subscriptions or to make them stop working for masters paying less than the recommended rate. Rattening was usually followed by a threatening letter signed by 'Mary Ann'.

4. The word 'snig' in Snig Hill probably refers to a block of wood that was used with cartwheels to act as a brake. As Snig Hill is on a steep slope that led to the town's manorial corn mill at Millsands, many a heavy load must have been braked on this steep hill.

5. A pointed knife for cutting and spearing food, of the sort that was made in Sheffield.

6. A 'Jennel'.

7. Butcher's Wheel on Arundel Street is one of the best of the few still surviving Victorian cutlery edge tool and file making works in Sheffield (see photograph S108709 on page 50). The brick-built works, extending to four storeys, was constructed in the mid 19th century by William and Samuel Butcher but incorporates an earlier works. Although now largely unused and awaiting renovation, it still exudes a sense of Dickensian working conditions. The large first and second floor casements were designed to shed maximum light on 'grinding hulls' that occupied those floors.

8. 'Crozzle', black, bubbly and with sharp edges, is often found topping walls throughout the Sheffield area, and was a by-product of the process by which blister steel was made in a cementation furnace (see also page 19). 'Crozzle' was the name given to the hard crust from the top of the sandstone chests containing iron bars covered by charcoal that were burned in the furnace.

9. The Sheffield Steelers.

10. Vulcan was the Roman god of fires and furnaces.

BUTCHER'S WHEEL, ARUNDEL STREET 2005 S108709

THE EX-ALFRED BECKETT'S BROOKLYN SAW WORKS 2005 S108720

THE CRIMEAN MONUMENT 1893 31962

NETHER EDGE ROAD AND POST OFFICE c1955 S108059

POST OFFICE
FRUIT
CAPSTAN
Toys

FRANCIS FRITH

PIONEER VICTORIAN PHOTOGRAPHER

Francis Frith, founder of the world-famous photographic archive, was a complex and multi-talented man. A devout Quaker and a highly successful Victorian businessman, he was philosophical by nature and pioneering in outlook. By 1855 he had already established a wholesale grocery business in Liverpool, and sold it for the astonishing sum of £200,000, which is the equivalent today of over £15,000,000. Now in his thirties, and captivated by the new science of photography, Frith set out on a series of pioneering journeys up the Nile and to the Near East.

INTRIGUE AND EXPLORATION

He was the first photographer to venture beyond the sixth cataract of the Nile. Africa was still the mysterious 'Dark Continent', and Stanley and Livingstone's historic meeting was a decade into the future. The conditions for picture taking confound belief. He laboured for hours in his wicker dark-room in the sweltering heat of the desert, while the volatile chemicals fizzed dangerously in their trays. Back in London he exhibited his photographs and was 'rapturously cheered' by members of the Royal Society. His reputation as a photographer was made overnight.

VENTURE OF A LIFE-TIME

By the 1870s the railways had threaded their way across the country, and Bank Holidays and half-day Saturdays had been made obligatory by Act of Parliament. All of a sudden the working man and his family were able to enjoy days out, take holidays, and see a little more of the world.

With typical business acumen, Francis Frith foresaw that these new tourists would enjoy having souvenirs to commemorate their days out. For the next thirty years he travelled the country by train and by pony and trap, producing fine photographs of seaside resorts and beauty spots that were keenly bought by millions of Victorians. These prints were painstakingly pasted into family albums and pored over during the dark nights of winter, rekindling precious memories of summer excursions. Frith's studio was soon supplying retail shops all over the country, and by 1890 F Frith & Co had become the greatest specialist photographic publishing company in the world, with over 2,000 sales outlets, and pioneered the picture postcard.

FRANCIS FRITH'S LEGACY

Francis Frith had died in 1898 at his villa in Cannes, his great project still growing. By 1970 the archive he created contained over a third of a million pictures showing 7,000 British towns and villages.

Frith's legacy to us today is of immense significance and value, for the magnificent archive of evocative photographs he created provides a unique record of change in the cities, towns and villages throughout Britain over a century and more. Frith and his fellow studio photographers revisited locations many times down the years to update their views, compiling for us an enthralling and colourful pageant of British life and character.

We are fortunate that Frith was dedicated to recording the minutiae of everyday life. For it is this sheer wealth of visual data, the painstaking chronicle of changes in dress, transport, street layouts, buildings, housing and landscape that captivates us so much today, offering us a powerful link with the past and with the lives of our ancestors.

Computers have now made it possible for Frith's many thousands of images to be accessed almost instantly. The archive offers every one of us an opportunity to examine the places where we and our families have lived and worked down the years. Its images, depicting our shared past, are now bringing pleasure and enlightenment to millions around the world a century and more after his death.

For further information visit: www.francisfrith.com

INTERIOR DECORATION

Frith's photographs can be seen framed and as giant wall murals in thousands of pubs, restaurants, hotels, banks, retail stores and other public buildings throughout Britain. These provide interesting and attractive décor, generating strong local interest and acting as a powerful reminder of gentler days in our increasingly busy and frenetic world.

FRITH PRODUCTS

All Frith photographs are available as prints and posters in a variety of different sizes and styles. In the UK we also offer a range of other gift and stationery products illustrated with Frith photographs, although many of these are not available for delivery outside the UK – see our website for more information on the products available for delivery in your country.

THE INTERNET

Over 100,000 photographs of Britain can be viewed and purchased on the Frith website. The website also includes memories and reminiscences contributed by our customers, who have personal knowledge of localities and of the people and properties depicted in Frith photographs. If you wish to learn more about a specific town or village you may find these reminiscences fascinating to browse. Why not add your own comments if you think they would be of interest to others? See **www.francisfrith.com**

PLEASE HELP US BRING FRITH'S PHOTOGRAPHS TO LIFE

Our authors do their best to recount the history of the places they write about. They give insights into how particular towns and villages developed, they describe the architecture of streets and buildings, and they discuss the lives of famous people who lived there. But however knowledgeable our authors are, the story they tell is necessarily incomplete.

Frith's photographs are so much more than plain historical documents. They are living proofs of the flow of human life down the generations. They show real people at real moments in history; and each of those people is the son or daughter of someone, the brother or sister, aunt or uncle, grandfather or grandmother of someone else. All of them lived, worked and played in the streets depicted in Frith's photographs.

We would be grateful if you would give us your insights into the places shown in our photographs: the streets and buildings, the shops, businesses and industries. Post your memories of life in those streets on the Frith website: what it was like growing up there, who ran the local shop and what shopping was like years ago; if your workplace is shown tell us about your working day and what the building is used for now. Read other visitors' memories and reconnect with your shared local history and heritage. With your help more and more Frith photographs can be brought to life, and vital memories preserved for posterity, and for the benefit of historians in the future.

Wherever possible, we will try to include some of your comments in future editions of our books. Moreover, if you spot errors in dates, titles or other facts, please let us know, because our archive records are not always completely accurate—they rely on 140 years of human endeavour and hand-compiled records. You can email us using the contact form on the website.

Thank you!

For further information, trade, or author enquiries please contact us at the address below:

The Francis Frith Collection, Frith's Barn, Teffont, Salisbury, Wiltshire, England SP3 5QP.

Tel: +44 (0)1722 716 376 Fax: +44 (0)1722 716 881

e-mail: sales@francisfrith.co.uk **www.francisfrith.com**